Who is speaking throughout these poems? The delight is in the blur: First-person becomes every-person, every-person a layered construct of past-and-present persons, and over all of this breathes the vast American West, which is itself a simultaneity—of time frames, landscapes, and cross-hatched journeys. Kevorkian's third poetry collection is redolent with history, especially the history of cultures' shifting claims over a region that remains resolutely itself—volcanic, untamable, partially mapped. Its laminate past is evoked through specific detail and moments of electrifying phrasing which nevertheless leave space for the reader to grasp not just a panorama of fleeting observations, but a tremendous intelligence at work.

~**LESLIE ULLMAN**, *Library of Small Happiness*

Reading *Quivira*, acute with restless shifting syntax and delineations as precise and startling as the "mottled sky a blue and white/cow blasting through broken window panes," one is captivated by the view, instantly recognizable and riven with sensibility. Encountering Karen Kevorkian's poems, one is caught up in an existential quest, both real and imagined, haunted by history and absence, driven by desire, "waking...to an "unseen/reliable trill" with "so many ifs and conditionals lying at your feet."

~**REBECCA SEIFERLE**, *Wild Tongue*

Karen Kevorkian's power resides in quiet ferocity, in her sunwetted "deviations of color/the mind like a desert a wheel turning," from the poet's hand to the live page where nature, the self, and politics can all become part of the same architectural vocabulary. Her latest book, *Quivira*, comes to us, "the body surprised," physically layered and incantatory as longing, as "hoarse horn bay cries," as certain sights like "lichenmottled rock." The book's overall lush, rapacious intelligence sees with the elegance of a wild animal at ease—in other words, Kevorkian has translated and become part of the literal, once metaphorical, landscape to create something philosophically beautiful.

~**ELENA KARINA BYRNE**, *Squander*

Also By Karen Kevorkian

Lizard Dream

White Stucco Black Wing

QUIVIRA

QUIVIRA

POEMS

Karen Kevorkian

THREE: A TAOS PRESS

Book Design & Typesetting: Lesley Cox, FEEL Design Associates, Taos, NM
Press Logo Design: William Watson, Castro Watson, New York, NY
Front Cover Artwork: *Hondo, 2017,* by Brian Shields, Oil, Gesso, and
Graphite on Canvas, artwork courtesy of the artist
Author's Photograph: Andrei Andreev, Los Angeles, CA

Text Typeset In: Metallophile Sp8 and Circe Slab C

Printed in the United States of America By Cottrell Printing Company

ISBN: 978-0-9994848-5-2

THREE: A TAOS PRESS
P.O. Box 370627
Denver, CO 80237

10 9 8 7 6 5 4 3 2 1

Contents

QUIVIRA

We Do Not Circumnavigate   13

I Would Have to Think of Others' Memories as My Own   14

Half-Unpacked Suitcase   16

Why Turn Around   17

Our Lady of Sorrows or Is It Solitude   18

Seem to Be Inscribing Some Sort of Language in the Air   19

The Mouth with the Gold Teeth Speaks   20

In the Mind, Synthesis   24

News from the Neighborhood of the Cave   25

When I'm Gone It's Finished, the Woman One of 65 Speakers of Kumeyaay   26

5 or 6 Miles Distant Rises a Gigantic Land Mass   28

Tin Wings on the Angelito   29

The Intervening Emptiness   30

All Deliberation Ceased   32

Barefoot and Naked Chosen for Goodness   33

Landscape Revealed by a Backward Glance   34

Clouds in the Sky, Electricity in the Atmosphere   36

Dark Red and Green   37

The Old Talpa Road   38

It Does Not Pass but Lingers   39

21 DAYS

21 Days   43

THE CALL AND THE DRAG

Explicit Comments About the West Coast, Non-Metaphorical   67

Evidently I Was Still Somewhere   68

I Became a Medicine Man 1   69

Once You Arrive on the Other Shore   70

This is the Land of Mirage   71

I Became a Medicine Man 2   72

Necrotopography   75

Her Nonchalant Way of Holding the Glass   76

After All These Years on Earth   77

The Sun Stabbing the Water the Wind Tugging at Her Dress   78

Dieric Bouts, Annunciation/Escola Flamega, *Annunciação/Gevelsteen,*

    De Annunciatie   80

Premonitions and Warnings We Give Ourselves   83

A Voice Immediately Familiar   84

There Was No Resistance   85

Black Cloth Far Away Stays With Me   86

Isla de Malhado   90

The Avocet   92

What Had Once Been My City   94

As Though to Die by Gunshot Were the Finest Play   96

And Yet I Find Myself Resisting   97

A Compelling Velvety Voice   98

Notes   99

Acknowledgments   103

About The Author   107

About The Artist   109

That they were not satisfied to think that there was no gold, on the contrary, they were of the belief it was to be found... .

No gold or silver was found among these people, nor information of any...

~PEDRO DE CASTAÑEDA DE NÁJERA

desire's manifest here, here, and here's
the infinite in the intervening emptiness

~ARTHUR SZE

QUIVIRA

We Do Not Circumnavigate

On hwy 40 crossing Arizona
shallow volcanic cones tenting not far
from road, now and then a coyote
      feet joined primly lay across a yellow stripe
soft pink earth eroding from a cliffside
announces a mesa's beginning

      easier in the mountains
not feeling in a fast car even trapped
by semis, call beautiful the narrow road
wall of angled rock you could touch
      on the other side the rushing green
ice cold Rio Grande, sense
of sudden passing upward into
particulate life

the gas furnace grunts into flame
in a quiet room, snow icily sheets
mud from the last storm, red furze
      shoots from stumps, rising then dying

turquoised fingers, a suitcase filled
with black clothes, the orange scarf you bought in
      Paris Athens Arequipa Santa Fe
that on waking you take milk and coffee
study a tree's mask of light
that there were a mother father grandparents uncles
aunts cousins mostly dead the lovers husbands
      self a wornout uniform all you had to put on

I Would Have to Think of Others' Memories as My Own

*...the magical name "Coronado...a talisman, a sign of mutual belief and promise
for people seeking their fortunes on Route 66*

~JOHN MILLER MORRIS

Pale green paloverdes feather Mojave
sideroads to Oatman, 130 miles to Needles
Land Sales, Yucca Proving Ground, gray boxcar
teeth strung across the despoplado
for we had not found
      the kingdom, foothills dropped from pinched
fingertips mottled sky a blue and white
cow blasting through broken windowpanes, million
year old basalt lavaspill three-bladed
windmills scything all the flowing, chamisa's
dirty smoke the white spark that lasts one hour
after waking
      I call you now everything
is rising, on concrete blocks rusted cars
and doublewides ceremonially
positioned
      they drew a line to keep us
from crossing over gave us headpieces
and dressed skins not gold and precious stones nor
brocades promised from the pulpit, we gave them
pearl beads cascabeles never seen before
heavy artillery and a good place to
batter down pueblos, looped aluminum
Xmas tinsel, human shielding,
      old firefilled
cottonwoods like hot air balloons at dusk
rising, with my ribboned tongue
I call you and what of it there is no
saving

      1000 horses 500 cattle 5000 sheep
1500 persons servants allies, the plains
leaving no more trace when we'd got through than
if no one had passed over, piled-up dung and
bones so the rear guard could follow
      short grass
after trampling stands up clean and straight again,
Styrofoam chest gouged with fingernail
halfmoons urinous sunsets breath
isn't it tired yet
      all that in and outness

Half-Unpacked Suitcase

I am a fierce driver making my miles
although four times sudden breaking
and pure luck saved me
            wrong turns onto rutted orange gravel
on the edge of the gorge a few feet away
a sheer riverdrop
                        the girl lay on the grass
head in the lap of a man drawing
charcoal designs on her chin, the chin
pricked in small even rows
with a sharp stick, the stick dipped in juice
of a certain river weed
then in the powder of blue stone
found in low water
                        fancied we were God's Israel
journeying to the Promised Land the red rock
yellow ochre sweeps tufts and spines
                  deviations of color
the mind like a desert a wheel turning
to dark night as it does
            feet's back and forth elegy
wailed formless words, acequias weedy
from brown sluggish riversluice
fire that cleans them

Why Turn Around

Houses that slickly incarnate pueblostyle smooth
imitation adobe the deep tan
of 1940s Max Factor pancake
       makeup worn until death
by the woman in Border nightclub
       tablesnaps her mouth the film star's
flared lipstick wings

Penitente Lane the strawflecked real adobe
refreshed yearly with soft red earth color

bright blue paint for shuttered
windows unused now no more cries

on a dirt path
       pawprints
strewn like flowers, owner's
sneaker treads always near

Our Lady of Sorrows or Is It Solitude

Each day contrives a new architecture of pillows
letters smoothed flat bent photos notes on yellow paper

whole years forgotten not necessarily the important ones

smudge by the door blueclad figure hovering
from the corner nattering a child who mumbles

out of adult hearing the voice always fictitious

hissy sibilants trees shushing stubby pile
of the almost velvet chair that looked smooth
prickles

8:30 p.m. too little light cat leads the way
disappears in gloom just above the floor

sensation of movement is what a ghost is worn sheets
and all the feet shoved to the end

Seem to Be Inscribing Some Sort of Language in the Air

You are walking on a side street
in a small western mountain town
opposite a muddy field where two horses
pasture you've walked past the horses before
today they are solemn not a wagging-tail day
          their eyes on pocks in the mud their hooves made
and you wanting the long lashes
of acknowledgment
                    a small cold wind
blows and a tree of brown leaves shakes
it is talking and the brown
rains down another gust
again that talking sound
the leaves give

like starlings, small black birds
of gold eyes that with one mind rise
from buildings or trees a tornado
to block light then fan and turn
a pointillist demotic

The Mouth with the Gold Teeth Speaks

The leaves here are gold
and the mornings so quiet
the heart thud
a startling sound
yet I do not think much
of my body

Patrociño Barela's carvings
prized not by his wife
who burned his night's work
for morning fuel

his dwarfsized La Muerte
sitting in a cart too big
to burn featureless
as a fetus that paradox
to be born is to die

heavy lidded the daubed saints
skinny Christs with those eyes
deep lines around the mouth
suggesting the sensual
of no use when nailed
to a cross except you
suffer majestically

in a chapel made of mud
where each year parishioners
refresh walls with more mud

the comforting surface
inviting to the hand
lively with bits of straw
the little church
in a fortresslike space

facing mountains the crosses
of derelict moradas
the phrase *cactus spine braided*
making space in the mind
with the practical small
basins in storerooms
to wash away blood

throw yourself against a body
to be forgiven if not
in the sense *God forgives you my child*
but physically shriven
as though the word
meant *peeled*

lain on the Earth's body
cushioned and weeping
adorned by the buzz
and lashes of remorse

like all the tattoos
acquired at the time
you believed your body
would always be firm

in the high desert Buddhists
speak of the murderous
Myanmar Buddhists whose
inhospitable treatment
of Muslims is grievous

the need to pick over many
contradictions

little bows
to each person speaking

an inky blue sky over boxlike
arid earth buildings
big rigs rolling down

the paseo also 4x4s, bikes
and those queuing for the free
plaza concert
with their children and dogs

arms and throats
arabesqued and limned

not just technique
this constant messing with
the specific, physical detail

gold trees are live coals
overhead it is rapture
you will be saved
any minute now

gain fluency in tongues
become supple and feel a rush
in the body absent
these many years

In the Mind, Synthesis

Thinking the day began well
when the magpie levitated through trees
      acute black and white
      delineating
a breast's small expanse
      the sun burnishing faces at certain angles
they could not refuse

saying then you also have the tattoos
and she slightly pulled down her sweater neck
      pointing to a dot in her cleft
saying there, that's one

arranged shelves, a corner fireplace beehive-molded
      kitchen gas heater on
turquoise Mexican oilcloth
splaying looselipped yellow roses

      it doesn't arrive just like that
the body surprised by each pendulum lunge
      the mask dropping
the silver one
although it was heavy
gorgeous

the heater turned itself off
      orchestration of thumps tings
tinny booming
shrill beauty, coyote or hound

News from the Neighborhood of the Cave

Spindly long limbs of chinese elms their howdy-do
of limp shadow nodding from the pavement

heat igniting her hair when she touched it
from the house a cat declared itself strangled

below lay a museum of layers geological so fragile
a bird's weightless landing could liquefy

(some did not turn faces toward sun preferring
the distorting world of the cave wall)

was she on fire what was it about shadow

When I'm Gone It's Finished, the Woman One of 65 Speakers of Kumeyaay

Left from a tribe in Mexico whose territory extended into California
            greeters of the Spanish in 1769 and maybe there
            1300 years before that or even thousands more
her children understand but don't speak it
            her grandchildren have lost it all
the cave where her family stayed
            moving in August between desert and sea
for the pine nut harvest taking two days on burro and foot
            up a shallow valley of silver sage and red shank
on the way greeting a cluster of dancing pines gone lost
            when animals
as well as trees were human

men hunting rabbits quail and deer
            children shaking branches
to knock down pine cones roasted for nuts
red shank could ease a toothache
            elderberry, a fever
                        buckwheat settled stomachs
whispers that wooly blue curls were for ladies
to tighten things up
            seem chaste

the granite of cave walls black with soot of hundreds
     maybe thousands of years of fire red clay shards
shattered underfoot
     the woman touches lichenmottled rock
speaks of family and friends, lights a sage bundle with a Bic
sweeping smoke, *Here you are still we've come to see you*
     I've brought a friend
to get to know you
     she cries and sings in Kumeyaay, sits a while
smoking a Marlboro drinking coffee from a thermos

5 or 6 Miles Distant Rises a Gigantic Land Mass

The daytime moon brighter than smooth horses
in the field on Kit Carson

a mudbricked house basketed by thin limbs
of almost bare aspens one called weeping
that hung to the ground
the limb's feathered yellow leaves
inviting rest
along a body's length

we knew of cities in flames
in defense of fictions

       near the great Saline cities of Abo, Qurai, Tabira
       (the Grand Quivira where Indians built for the padres
       a church of rose and tan like a rattlesnake)

words slipped side to side, lachrymatories, containers for tears

tenebrous, pitchdark

       I cannot tell you what country this is
       for I think it is not on the map
       the general said

Tin Wings on the Angelito

Face at a window, thuds against the wall, wooden chairbacks lit up
with varnish like syrup

rain finally fallen, air's odor of shirts seldom washed

the time for civility and dissemblement, twilight's threadbare hour

no clouds or haze to soften the Oh I don't know whatever
you take it to mean

so many ifs and conditionals lying at your feet

The Intervening Emptiness

Sun hot on the face body numb
in its fleece
white dry leaf flung up by the foot

a brown rabbit so large
character from a folktale

waiting for the rapture

trees that disappear into
smoke of their own dryness
figure in an orange coat
walking down the road
       o my love why
hast thou

       sky a gray cloth
resting on the blue ridge
I've heard of a sacred lake
that I, so white,
can't see

Bears Ears shrinking
who remembers Church Rock

largest release of
radioactive
material in
American history
the

still-high uranium
levels in Arizona
tap water

nothing much
in the photo

Navajo man in foreground
the road's long perspective
shrunk, a pinpoint

not too far away
volcanic upsurge of the high desert
layered contrasts orange and coral

All Deliberation Ceased

Declare that I own one ass and a pitchfork

that I own a loom with its threads and a screw

that I have a house consisting of eight rooms a porch and four ruined rooms

that I have 14 gilded images 2 old carts and a spit to roast meat on

that I own six beef cows with one calf that is suckling a tame burro

that I procreated eighteen children and of these seven survive

that I was never married but always single

that I have five she goats and one small one

that Don Francesco Montoya owes me a dagger with Our Lady of Sorrows on it

that when I got married she had no assets and neither did I we were both poor

that I own a small Chinese pot that is at the house of Feliciano Ulibarri

that I own a pair of gold earrings and one piece of crinoline to be sold for masses

that I own a chest with a key

that I own my clothing which I used: two pair of woolen pants, three (I mean four)

jackets or waistcoats, on of blue cloth of second quality, when I say first quality

I mean lined two of satin and one of black baize, a blue cloth cape of second

quality and five jackets, one of hand-embroidered cloth

that I was married according to the Catholic Church but my wife abandoned me

that I do not recognize her as having any rights to my property

that I have one pregnant burro

that I have the one she burro and one pistol that has six shots in it

that I own one half of a house and an apricot tree

that I wish to be buried in the cemetery like a pauper

Barefoot and Naked Chosen for Goodness

No wind yet the flame of the outdoor heater's nimbus
blew out not one time, twice
       on Quesnel's little field the sunwetted horses
can you doubt your god's
intentions
dry lands offer the means to scourge
       thorny crowns made from canes of wild roses
       canyon walls streaked by manganese, dark paint
that chimes nearblack from the smooth
       Cristo with thorns and waistcloth
red circles on each knee red paint on brow.
       smiling Death in a wooden cart
       row of teeth in painted mouth
real hair
hanging
lank

Landscape Revealed by a Backward Glance

Against white snow the brown movement
absorbed by dark tangles of winter deadleaf
   coyote
making furtive risky
pass through town
then the pigsize rabbit

treelimbs aroil
a little smokier
than yesterday
oh bunny
   cuidado

last night the novelist asked
had others the right to tell
his story
a crisp no he said
afterwards
the arguments:
imagination/appropriation
my story/his story
her story/my story
too white

in the local museum
plenty whiteguy views of pueblos
the Couse paintings
like the Curtis photos

locals posed in costume
for Southern Pacific calendars
for the taste of Eastern tourists
looking down from trains
eating up
the picturesque

beloved Frank Waters telling the Hopi
story, more ethnography than
fictive writing more fictive writing
than ethnography

less a thought than spectral
as snow that won't melt

coyote's way of being
not there
there
making you want
        the real fourlegged
roughcoated sharpnosed
        that comes and goes

don't make too much of it
        I'm not from the pueblo
no more than the way a car idling
in cold robes itself in a white cloud

Clouds in the Sky, Electricity in the Atmosphere

Kitchen sink hot water mechanical
rinsing the red pool that in last night's
glass made a scab

somewhere else to pack up from
rituals of the good guest stripped bedsheets fridge emptied
sink scoured leave no hairs DNA cops
ready with your crimes

in the dream of uncovered bodies
the father weeping the sudden twig to a tall thin boy
so mockingly looking down
someone of interest and why hadn't I
called those
who should know

in dark's glare the least chair or table
seemed cozied with snow

and when the flakes did fall finally
it was lazily
blue juniper berries
stiff adorning

Dark Red and Green

It was the year of girls enameling toenails black
what made it a special day a man kneeling on a roof
his hammer echoing across a field
redly arid small houses rapacious trees
a body creased from tossed sheets the overhead fan
unsettling gray ceiling ferment
        water rusted from a tap dishes clinked syllables
spires of grass gave stately side to side
        a bee left a flower to return to the same pale ear
to rise dust laden
        grief fluttering
sunlight full on it

in the corn dance boys shifted
tall stalks in a row of stalks smoke alive in hair
certain rise and fall of feet mechanically the women
beat time with bunched grass the quicker and younger boys
shook gourds loose with seed
        each old man carried one drum
all the world needed to complete winding rows of the dance
        its turns and returns
foxtails bounced at the boys' waists
in the hair of each a tentative feather
        seeking pith the obsidian water
slashed beneath wooden planks
sunlight made parchment of hackberry leaves
        whuh uhn huh woed a dove
too much green
        relief at a red car passing

The Old Talpa Road

Slowing on the old Talpa road
for a guidebook-listed softshouldered mudbricked church
        of dim timbered ceiling and painted reredos
little mustached saints' bedroomy eyes

a locked family chapel Our Lady of Talpa
        two dogs barking
        but the day is warm and
sleepily they slouch to earth

take a cellphone picture

broken into after 200 years
        the blackeyed saints sold
        Virgins of Dolores and Conception of triangled stiff skirt
to a Colorado collector
        the family then mostly gone or cash-strapped

before the whole altar lost they let it go
they way they do

one side collapsed
        big mud bricks fallen
in the photo the patriarch a witness

at 16 death seemed improbable
laughed you'd kill yourself at 30
        no one then was that old
time is what there is
plenty of

It Does Not Pass but Lingers

Unaccustomed in this dry land to mud left by snow
the gray crust it leaves on hems of long pants
its packing into shoe treads

reading more is coming

the air in California very bad now finding
remains from the fire corridors of firestripped treetrunks
husks of cars in lines on the roads
ash sifted
yellow air

what an idea trying to outrun
the fire
in a moment
on you

in this bronze and berried land
this white blanketed land
oh get it right its
filigreed tall trunks gilded

21 DAYS

As if the streets were the barrels of multiple telescopes trained on the desert, on the planted fields, on the scrubland and pastures, or on the bare hills that on moonlit nights seemed to be made of bread crumbs.

~ROBERTO BOLAÑO

21 Days

1   *The Pilgrim*

Everything had been a lie
walking 1100 miles to what
upright truth standing on its head
trickster, gulling

       22 pounds on her back. Choosing
whether to eat or
carry weight
               rising 3 a.m. to walk into milk
of the Andromeda galaxy old
sidelying universe, pointing to the east
she followed it
          compostela
a field of stars   drenched
in them

       what was the lie
           steps scattered with straw
replaced by gravel paths of old Roman roads
Pyrenees crossed in a rainstorm, path

the mountain filled with fast rushing water
       deep mud each step
sucking down her shoes a laughing sound

2   *High Desert*

November sun the horizon's
laserlight concludes
the dry plain. Conical anthills
lacking industry, big red ants
a summer bounty. Cedar posts
and barbed wire *bobwire*
they called it
       along the path
at intervals
       rocks in disarray
a pattern that had meant
something, intention

3   *Where Is the Path*

The yellow roadstripe slightly curving
lent to tan buildings with turquoise
wood shutters a Christina's world
moment but she wasn't crawling
        gobsmacked by silence that
emptying toward someone or something
        inert for days like fog not
the precipitous kind
        that descended Nob Hill from Grace
wet dusk icelike on cheeks
        to the Embarcadero where ghosts
of shipping and cruise lines receded
in felted night
        in bed in the little room
window raised just enough to hear
announcement
        of hoarse horn bay cries
not asking
where is the path but why
                inside the heaviness

4

Let me tell you
about this dark
           like a bruise
the fist you didn't see
                    naked in Klieg light
giant merciless tambour

is that what was done wrong
              binaries
a bright bladed knife

eyes on her
                    something new

5

The cat's black velvet sizzles with cold
come in come in
stranger to me
with your gold eyes
I myself love a mask
sometimes very tired
take it off

dry aspen leaves she
brings in
curled
yellow tongues

6

Little mudded wall only chest high
the leaves obediently
shore against you
               in the thick limbs
of the tall cedar black-and-white
birds clack insanely
for blue berries
        such a thrashing

7

Sky streaked pink as eyelid rims
oh I said seeking   not
rapture but close to it (train
not pulling into)

the mesa's disarranged
stones behind the morada
among each heap
a number painted on one stone
to number 14   the Stations

chamisa veering yellowish
and silver dust   dark blue
scalloping hills   No
Trespass Tribal Lands   No
Hunting   No
Woodcutting   such
are the given signs

8

Pink roses spun on walls I was
made of piano keys
you pressed them you said

your black silk shirt your
hooded eyes I said the upturned
corners of your lips

here is dry land from which bloom
tall cottonwoods yellow aspens
gold and silver scrub
          made from dust
absence
to be grateful for

oh I said if that's how you feel
let me demonstrate
my elegant
turning away form

9

        He'd said I am climbing the tree
through the interlace   a city
        pale towers as backstory
of the Ghent altarpiece in Saint Bavo where the lamb
stands in the meadow and far away
the nearly transparent towers rise
        there is no tree in the painting

gold leaf raised by a comb
run through hair
the thin sheets of it
statically cling

tremble over adhesive
square after square

burnished the stars
on a blue robe gleam

10

Morning the sheen of
camposanto grass speaks

tired from upthrusting
mounds of yellow dirt
clumping small fenced
territories

to say a life its

Walmart flowers
angels plaster and plastic
toy trucks seashells toy sheep
opened concrete bibles
blue gowned virgin in a little cage

faded red white and blue flags limp
at government-paid-for stones

wine bottles dropped in an urn
winter solstice skies
porcelain blue

names of the leftbehinds
on newer stones

earth from a rotating
space station a small planet
of notable chemistry
discernible patterns

11

        The overland trail lined with graves
a dying daughter begging the men to dig
down 6 feet so the wolves
would not find her
        the tired men
reaching 4 feet that's enough
the mother
grabbing a shovel jumping into the grave
        covering it with cactus

so much sky here at night comes through
the ceiling
stars waver in the dark room
heavy quilts layered on the bed

red ant on cone of yellow dirt
a woman arranging stones
or a young man bent under weight
of a wooden cross
that drags the ground
theatrics of living

left at the graves pink rosary
for protection
lady
in a blue cape

drone of music at bedside
in the dark little
bottle
of water
nightlight
book
balm

12

Thumb and index lightly
pinching releasing
the soft ear of the
black cat then lightly
roughly squeezing
her nape

not purring you know
this is not how she
is used to touch

but holding still
something
to learn

that first
motel night in
my white slip knowing
I did not feel the way
he said my name for
this I send back my
apology

13

The Aztec dancers wear exotic purchased feathers
(no longtailed birds on the Paseo)
choreography in the motel foyer where
a velvety Santa says
What can I bring you for Xmas little girl

that hour on the highway late day sun
blasts an ability to see as if
powering such motorized tonnage
a silly idea

14

Warm cedar stench
a small fan of it crushed in the pocket
maybe 15 then
taking a drive
bleak stone and scrub
the new world
Texas Xmas day
cards' white blanketed houses
choristers who held open scores
pillowed chimneys
emotional stars

driving without thinking to arrive
although soon to turn toward
his house my house stunned rooms

sky too warm day too long little tables
with dishes of ribboned
hard candies

15

Black patent sky
snow's crisp talking back

car's cold cave breath
rimed at the curb
5000 feet
scalding light of the box store

boil water with chocolate and sugar
simmer with milk until heavy
in a white china cup

small room with one chair for reading
white noise in the mind a cat tongue's
soft clicks wetting fur

waking in stilldark
to an unseen
reliable trill

16

The last day
like peering into a glass case
turquoise and silver

small town with streetlights
only now and then turned on
dark to hurry through
passing the little horse field
cars parked at the fringe

17

The high road it's called whether
you drive up or down
in wet snow the mud becomes glass
you will fishtail
slide into a curve around
a steep drop
a boy comes by in his flatbed
how do I
get out of here
just hold on
drive

18

In the Mojave
car windows rolled up
you know it's windy
the creosote
bushes lean hard
to one side

shores of red dirt
arroyos erode in
vertical channels
little topographies

jawbone my bone
ivorying teeth

ground down worried
little hollows

19

Almost no buildings on the way
to burning Los Angeles

turning off the highway to find
Desert Information
road a perforated map line
meaning gravel or dirt

a country crossed in wagons
directed by gravemounds
cairned with rocks
so the wolves wouldn't

20

The jigger of the present
the steady power
of the hours
what it sounds like

in the desert
facing east in the morning
crack from a tree limb
flesh becoming

curved swift of absence
Frankenstein
to bring life to

what it sounds like
crow clacker
thigh slapper
ash shimmerer
cough faded to rasp

21

Pink torn scarves the sky's antidespair

red fire ants
        exquisitely fine baskets
                yucca sandals for the long trek

you feel very far away   I am
        1000 miles   can you hear me
            are you there

the pueblo's pale ochre
mounds toward San Jose de Laguna
        blue smoke upstreaming fenced yard dogs in and out
the altar's painted ceiling stars
        one white woman
capable of quiet

THE CALL AND THE DRAG

Explicit Comments About the West Coast, Non-Metaphorical

Santa Monicas and San Gabrielinos backdrop the city
she once called her Gran Quivira

where men strap on leaf blowers yank cords hard
wave wands left and right in priestly benison

fantasies of Spanish stucco and red tile nod to
European slaughter over transsubstantive mysteries

shifting cutlery of green palms
hillside pumpjacks that bow and rebow in dinosaur feasting

where someone waving arms at another means I Am Done
a laddered sidewalk cartography of a new mappa mundi

acetylene rattats of crows whose feathers are not lustrous
or secretive but inarticulate as the black of old coffee

beneath streets' gridded logic a river's liquid cursive
the green silk across around returning

red neon hand of a Psychic Life Coach
pendulum swing of a windowblind
cord lapping in circles now

Evidently I Was Still Somewhere

After 7 hours in bed not always with closed eyes
it's 6 a.m.

lifting a hot cup, chewing an apple

daylight gleaming colorlessly on a car hood

a hamster's life you call purposeful

photo of the aged Duras at her desk a place
I always thought to arrive

now I am that and time
a pack of cards at my back

Riding in a car, someone opening the door, saying
And?

And? I replied, whatever it was, he wanted to hear it

I Became a Medicine Man 1

I the most daring and reckless of all

~ALVAR NUÑEZ CABEZA DE VACA

I'm the sphinx on the pediment of sand looking east into the sun
        it began to rain and the sea toughened
                after midnight the sound of many voices
                tinkling little bells also flutes and tambourines
                until the storm ceased
the way you come to a place thinking you won't stay long
        the little boat on top of treetops
                the disfiguring rocks
a place unfamiliar for years until one day it isn't
        told I could be of help
        by breathing on the sick
                with that breath and my hands
                drive ailments away
the way I lift a pen quickly from a page and without much intention
yields an imprint of the almostthought
        the one who kept me said had I so much power
        I would not suffer so
                arriving from the sea
                I was surely wiser
an armada of standing paddleboarders sometimes slides under
sunlight repents on the chop of water
        every stone in the field, heated, had its use
                took away pain
        I cut open a breast with a stone knife
                the arrowhead begged
                the entire village lined up to touch it
elegantly what is here is not there
        in the ragged terms of the place
                a believing army
many adept at riding the waves others
in the deep troughs

Once You Arrive on the Other Shore

Yellow smiley face aloft
        from parasail a body dangles
not far away the swimmers' circle
ceremonializes ashes
        saltfilled mouths
send spit to ocean corridors
        (the other
great blue river banked
with white paperpetalled roses)

boogieboard seller drags sand
        rasprasping
girls rope oily seakelp
        swoopbreasted women
sashay pigeonpurple
gorgets chiming

oh no he says I didn't mean it that way
highstepped gulls
        transpose
cuneiform sandtracking

This Is the Land of Mirage

Down the hill from the mission garden
of downturned trumpets and
spattered white blades
of sicksweet datura
the saved long deep dirt trough
where waterweighted cloth
pulled down Chumash arms
evermoving as the bluegreengray Pacific
in the chapel a mouth hailing Mary
stone robes swinging clothlike
candle flames struggling
against dust's perpetual hour
darkclotting the high ceiling
coins clink for a candle taken
from a corded choir
wicktipped flaming
squat base dug in sand
a man comes with a bucket
his job to yank free all
the candles whether stumps or tapering
at the ocean's edge the Chumash
said to call out make room

I Became a Medicine Man 2

Lace pattern of salt in the spent waves
farther out cresting, melonveined

       all they killed they set before me not
       daring to touch it even if
       dying of hunger unless I first blessed it

on the sand enacting my part

       little boys with long knotted wet hair
           thighdeep in water, watching it mount
           assess the moment it will befriend them

older, older now he mouths
turns his sealblack wetsuited body
staggers through cursive water

       how a light wind lifts sand
           the bent and broken bristled gull feather

gray and dirty crossing the shore
then blue and green uttering tongues
indeterminate and dark

it was tiresome
        to have to breathe on and make the sign of the cross

purple but like most things
that wasn't it either

        so it is easy to realize how greatly we were bothered
                the women bringing us
                tunas spiders worms

        whatever else they could find

shore skimming flocks
though *flock* carries inside too much of the guttural
shimmer like thought
in cloudy suspension

        as soon as they touched my body
                those who received me returned
                to their houses on a run
                then came again

or if I did not like what I saw in the eyes
turned my head pretending I had not seen

        wanting something of someone
                if I could not find the words
                could not look at the faces directly

alone and isn't that what was wanted

      many beads and robes of cowskin
      taking care of them as best I could. Meaning

a good night no hours of churning unease

      reaching their houses I found them seated
         faces turned to the wall

         belongings gathered in a heap on the floor
         heads bowed and hair pulled over the eyes

my own dry idiom

Necrotopography

Brutal necklaces of shells around each grave

~HART CRANE

The shape exactly
of an inverted boat
the long barrow

assembled mounds
resembling
shoals of minnows

clam cowrie cockle and conch
boiled white

cover them
exactly

Her Nonchalant Way of Holding the Glass

Pressed against a porch wall to keep out of busy gray rain
although bare armed and bare legged not shy of it

prismatically shifting tissue thin wet hydrangeas
clumped compactly as brains

oh beautiful ditherer   drenched and feeling changed

looking left looking right quickly drinking one glass
then another then washing the glass

The body as if trampled on in wet soft mud in which
deep prints of heavy boots remain

their sucking sounds

rain does not leave the face alone

dripping from the hat closing the eyes cool sliding past lips

inside the heavy canvas coat the arms try to raise themselves
but the wet coat is of such weight the arms cannot rise

After All These Years on Earth

Rescue boats wrap
migrant bodies
in gilt blankets
festive as chocolates

take me to the river
dip me in the water
I want to know

eyes head hands shift
legs cross uncross music
the flow

The Sun Stabbing the Water the Wind Tugging at Her Dress

In front of the apartment house El Sueño del Mar a woman of plaster
on a hint of a lawn psyche knot at her nape dress asymmetrically
draped and bunched at the waist

studied her new hand swollenfingered like a Mickey Mouse glove

all spring she'd examined the same wrist's extruded rebar dogged scrutiny
of absence

who would do that and didn't you shiver the body obedient to mind
the rebar so bonelike at the end of the white plaster flesh of her arm
mired in agapanthus

a hundred florets clustered in a drooping heavy head their blue
the promised one where the sun's pink flatline slid into the Pacific
she might have followed

the Via Sacra to the foot of the Acropolis shaking branches above her head
for the exultant rasp

buying a diet coke and those slippers with hairy yarn pom poms
tutuwearing soldiers prance in

fingered blue amulets to protect from the evil eye protection glassy
as a lover's kisses planted here and here on the back and the ass

money in the bank like her castdown glance the prey of those
passing fast with tight smiles

like Daphne laurelizing her best possibility as she sought the place
where the mystery would be known

although it proved to be some business about the mind's wellbeing or
the soul influenced by the body such things were contingent
what was skin anyway

a street strewn with starpetalled flowers of white oleander
a cream cup of magnolia furled fetally
that bruised when she placed on her eyes dark coins of glass

change was to slip into the sea a warm body inching into cold that
crossable edge his idea of foreplay

slap and a twist
all spring she examined the dark metal prongs extended
from the white plaster arm

as a few crows pecked in the little yard of blue flowers beyond them
tireless waves and arms' angular flashing

Dieric Bouts, *Annunciation*/Escola Flamega, *Annunciação/Gevelsteen, De Annunciatie*

1

Stark the hand
on blue silk luster
        not a dress you could wear
for any event, a drapery, tablecloth, disguise

In reply:
        a cot or bench near the wall where
red cloth puddles, the angel's
motley wings angels often wear
in these moments

through the window sitting on a wall
a peacock, dully
a few buildings a riverbank
trees of toothpicky bark

If I knew what to say she'd say
how to react I am trying to
love him say something of myself
oh never mind what to do with this

2

Less us than his idea of us
a role hard to play

all dead now all of them

the ones in the room
the ones waiting at home
someone else someone else
woman I told my secrets to
secrets now safe

3

        the skeptical Marys
the angel importuning
its colored feathers that make
banners of wings
not instruments of flight

sussurous murmurs fan
like wings of green parrots
that flew down from
the juniper
expectantly

half turned surprised
by what has entered her small room
private from the look of it
always an open window
and a book

the window usefully glimpsing a city
to go to if you don't have to keep
your angel date
the propositioning

someone else's dream an abstraction
that glory or duty like most things
lead to
the knife cuts the bleeding
the very small room

Premonitions and Warnings We Give Ourselves

Winter light bluish like skim milk
couples with strollers and golden retrievers
the old in sensible shoes and unflattering hats

as if an alarm sounds green dogwood seeds redden

eight or nine loud pops but looking outside
there is nothing   a ring rolls on the floor

hard hands   wet grass   little bites of fire in the dark

Dido holding a shallow cup
to tip out wine between horns of a white shining heifer

what good
are vows and shrines   dust each month layers as it sifts

fingers of light splay and slide down a wall
open doors into a rug's misshapen hexagons
zealous triangles of red

A Voice Immediately Familiar

Outside 7 a.m. the spiraldownward shrill, as if hawks spoke Mandarin

saying *xie xie*

the drawn out ee thanking air, the leafy ordinary

one came to the porch, looked down at the fat lounging cat

I waved my arms

the first time to really see it

usually nested in the green of the chinese elm

a name I am sure of, unlike the name

I can't find for the hawk

its call not matching descriptions in Peterson

photographed from underneath, wings outstretched in flight

the bird would have to die for me to see that

my daughter, at her father's, waits to name what is left

two turkey buzzards, yesterday

caped in long gray feathers, settling on the roof of his house

such a harbinger

too obvious, for his long dying that will surprise no one

least of all the one who sees in a corner

what others can't, filling a grocery store shopping bag,

pajamas, tobacco, clean shorts, saying not yet

There Was No Resistance

There was no resistance she said for the first time
she could slip her fingers into his grasp

the hand the softest she had ever felt it

his family gathered at the bed she leaned down whispered
I know you don't like them I don't either

then it was all business

I'm ok she said *I got it all out*

a hot day, hawks eee eee eee, what's left of a bird
on the brown mulch wing feathers and torqued spine

agony of dismembering

largemouthed plastic bags in the house

from the roof pinsharp eyes watching
dark rustle of wings heaving to rise

candor of talons
curved over roof edge

will it come back to eat it

the last few days they could not understand what he said when the nurse
changed him he still had his modesty pointing to the daughter
then the door—*You*— *over there*

the hawk guarding what it left how a cat shows you

Black Cloth Far Away Stays with Me

which ripens from nothing
~MIGUEL HERNÁNDEZ

People washed the body stuck it
told it to open wide to ease
the pill down the dry throat

sometimes necessary to turn
from eyes sometimes dust
settling on shoulders
of ornamental glass

not tall brown important bottles
with white plastic caps

tilting toward a mirror's
long silver shafts
slant like rain

the body
almost no more it
drifted on opiate seas
it left the shore
what good

was disappointment
or relief pale as
longstalked lilies'
sickest sweetness

eyelet edging
the pillowy quilt
bunched so like
a watchful dog
ready for
come here now

~

Lowspread live oak leaves
rattle money in a cup
whitewings teeter
on powerlines
soft music their call
hesitates between
first tones and last

a middle place lasting
seven days though such
long days what
absurdity

are the leaves solid black
gauze sky pushed into a room
where TV bodies
lie oddly angled
in blooming red fire

deafness within deafness
smoke in the night fireflies
sparking what is rough
what is smooth what are
their names *mind of*
clear light

~

Twisting below streets
a river sunburned with rust

here and there its
banana tree thickets
wet moss and urine
tuneless flagstone
underfoot

above hotel workers
waited for buses
organized walking to
buildings no longer standing
here is where once
every sentence began

~

Miguel Hernández
certain Pablo
Neruda needed
to hear

the nightingale
in dark climbed a tree
whistling

shown mouth
in a half grin
jaw-binding
band of cloth
teeth like a child

nights
rats did not
fear him
days he lay in sun

one corner of
the prison yard
a grave he said rid
him of loving

Isla de Malhado

every bone could be counted

~ALVAR NUÑEZ CABEZA DE VACA

When green the milk of prickly pears
burned the mouth

surviving on worms
ant eggs lizards poisonous snakes
even those with tail tips like
little horny pods
that shook like castanets

others stranded so hungry they ate each other up
until one left alone
who had no one to eat him

why think of this coast where
kids in subtropical dark will
run toward planktonstarred waves
the adults in too bright rooms
sharing drinks over
small kitchen tables

they rub tomatoes on
red shoulders to
suck out the sting

eskimo pies at the pier's end
yield chocolate shells'
teethnumbing hearts

naked and unused to it
they shed skin two times a year
the way serpents did

rescuers, overcoming their
first fears, lay hand on the
strangers' faces
then their own

as if the heat of another's body
could explain the mystery
of their separation

The Avocet

A beach slopes to where packed sand
is coolly kind and riptides
suck water into tall waves
tugging feet down into
the call and the drag

the ebbing called back into curl
creation physics the random
turned in on itself

onelegged an avocet sleeps
head turned 180
long beak buried
in feathered back furrow
one eye always watching

a man's raised arms
as green water rises
higher on his chest
ask waves not to hit him

the swimmer
propelled over swells
cocooned in water
irrefutable solitude

onshore mansized kelp
unrolls ragged unravel

Cabeza de Vaca left Cádiz
in 1527
2 ships 300 men 4 survivors
stranded

castaways no longer
but explorers
2 kids make for water crabwise

a woman's long skinny braids
enact schoolgirl myth of the
broadbrimmed sombrero

hands on hips for camera
the body thinks it knows
the avocet waiting
soft and gray as a cat

What Had Once Been My City

A funerary tower halfway climbed
the Bedouin on a little motorbike always ahead at the next site
necklaces looped on his arm swinging

the teenaged executioners parading in front of bound prisoners
before two-thousand-year-old temple columns
which at that moment still rose

instructed to accept *the cruelty that is wartime* its ochre horizon

some believing the border wall slows down large groups
others having little faith in it

in earliest life forms the human body took shape
predator fishes with long spines thick boney arms
protostarfish like meadow grasses in a breeze accepting
what came along in the current

a land where people did everything
with little flint knives set in wooden handles
who sharpened blades rapidly against their own teeth
like monkeys who put everything in their mouths

a man chides in low tones the large dog he holds on his lap
the dog moving closer until its body is one with the master's

I take all jurisdiction, civil as well as criminal, high as well as low
from the edge of the mountains to the stones and the sand in the rivers
and the leaves on the trees

on snow beside a mountain lake a woman's skin spasmed
from the cold she called *pure*
naked body gray in the water's dusk

years solder solid black scrolled linoleum or paper
like something saved from the flames of Alexandria's library

remember Ahkmatova's *I can*, a lightning strike
on desert sets a glass web in the sand

As Though to Die by Gunshot Were the Finest Play

In Ciudad Juárez where
some worship Santa Muerte

skeletal santa of death the public
cemetery teems and putresces

      some deaths summon
ten-foot-tall angels in white
gowns and feathers silver paint
in hair

      metal folding chairs screech
as they climb on
    apparitions
        children
blanks
    driven fast
to the place of killings

the unbroken
yellow highway stripe uncloses
Chihuahua desert quiet
      too large
white wings loft from the pickup bed
    splay
in the wake

And Yet I Find Myself Resisting

Fell asleep on the sand, woke to skinheat
and chasmed quiet
stone that could not be made wretched

his detecting wand perusing shoreline
a man picks up a small thing
pockets it

in rage a child's body lifts from ground
fistfuls of sand flung at gulls
their indifferent rising

the ocean exhaling a gathering swell
what's incoming surges
over seakelp, fetally knotted

surfers on boards sit sentry
to waves heaved upright
then the diagonal slither

A Compelling Velvety Voice

Dust fine as talc unfragranced and pale, a road
eerily untrafficked though now and then

disordered by cars, overhead the cold pearl of the moon
and thudding film memory

where a biplane's cutting-off engine struggled through
smoke of dawn dying in bare daylight

if not directly over the roof under which people slept
then close enough *my darling*

is it too late
up and down the road doors slamming

the small plane disturbing crows' sleek unseen bodies
sheen of feathers uprising

Notes

The name Quivira continued to be featured on maps into the 17th century. In making that name the book title, I wanted to address, to quote Carl Phillips, "how any myth/is finally about the lengths the mind will/carry a tale to, to explain what the body//knows already, and so never answers" ("Teaching Ovid to Sixth-Graders," *Cortège*, 1995).

The first inhabitants of North America left records in architecture, culture, artifacts, and markings on the landscape. They also are present in the written records dating from the 16th century by Spanish explorers, whose quests for fantastic treasure more often yielded spectacular failures. Under the twinned banners of promised wealth for themselves and spiritual salvation for those they conquered, their punishing explorations brought to native people the devastating consequences of contact.

Two of these written accounts resonated in making the poems in this book: the vivid *Narrative of the Coronado Expedition,* by Pedro de Castañeda de Nájera, ed. John Miller Morris (Chicago: R.R. Donnelly & Sons, 2002), which includes the English translation of the manuscript by George P. Hammond and Agapito Rey [1940]. In 1540 Francisco Vásquez de Coronado led a large-scale expedition from Mexico across the Southwest in the quest for gold to rival that found by Hernán Cortés in his 1521 conquest of the Aztec empire. The treasure was said to be found in Quivira, one of the fabled Seven Cities of Cíbola, although when located in what is now Kansas, only found were thatched houses and fields of corn, beans, and squash.

A similarly detailed account was written by Alvar Nuñez Cabeza de Vaca, *The Narrative of Cabeza de Vaca [La Relación,* 1542], ed. and trans. by Rolena Adorno and Patrick Charles Pautz (Lincoln: University of Nebraska, 2003). He tells of his experience with the ill-fated Narváez expedition that set out from Spain in 1527 for Mexico but went aground in Florida. Its survivors, ultimately four out of approximately 300, made their way to the coast of Texas, wandering there and in northern Mexico for eight years. Cabeza de Vaca's journal offers the earliest European depiction of the vast expanse of continental North America, notably foregrounding the customs and interactions of native people.

In addition to these journals, the poems in this book reference the following:

In "Quivira," part 1:

The epigraph is from Arthur Sze, "The Unfolding Center," *The Compass Rose* (Port Townsend: Copper Canyon, 2014). "Half-Unpacked Suitcase" refers to a captivity narrative by Margot Mifflin, *The Blue Tattoo: The Life of Olive Oatman* (Lincoln: University of Nebraska, 2009). "The Mouth with the Gold Teeth Speaks" mentions Patrociño Barela (1900–1964), whose *Carreta de La Muerte,* a wood sculpture, is in the collection of the Harwood Museum, Taos, NM; the title is taken from Charles Wright, "Nine-Panel Yaak River Screen," *A Short History of the Shadow* (New York: Farrar, Straus Giroux, 2002). "5 or 6 Miles Distant Rises a Gigantic Land Mass" refers to the ruins of an abandoned pueblo in New Mexico that has been given the name La Gran Quivira, part of the Salinas Pueblo Missions National Monument. "The Intervening Emptiness" refers to "Church Rock Tailings Spill: July 16, 1979," website of the New Mexico Office of the State Historian. "All Deliberation Ceased" (a cento) is based on Henrietta M. Christmas and Patricia S. Rau, comp. and ed., *Probates & Wills, Santa Fe, New Mexico, 1774–1896* (Los Ranchos, NM: Rio Grande Books, 2012). "Landscape Revealed by a Backward Glance" mentions E. Irving Couse (1866–1936), first president of the Taos Society of Artists; Edward S. Curtis (1868–1952), whose photography focused on the American West; and Frank Waters (1902–1995), who for 50 years wrote novels and historical works about the American Southwest.

In "21 Days," part 2:

The epigraph is taken from Roberto Bolaño, *Woes of the True Policeman: A Novel,* tr. Natasha Wimmer (New York: Farrar, Straus Giroux, 2011).

In "The Call and the Drag," part 3:

The epigraph for "Necrotopography" is from "O Carib Isle," *The Complete Poems and Selected Letters and Prose of Hart Crane,* ed. Brom Weber (New York: Liveright, 1966). "Premonitions and Warnings" makes reference to Robert Fitzgerald's translation of *The Aeneid,* book 4 (New York: Random House, 1983). "Annunciation" mentions in the title Dieric Bouts (1415–1475). "Black Cloth Far Away Stays with Me" refers to Spanish Civil War poet Miguel Hernández (1910–1942), "I Move Forward in the Dark" ["Sigo en la sombra, lleno de luz"], *Miguel Hernandez: Selected and Translated by Don Share* (New York: NYRB, 2013). "To Die by Gunshot Is the Finest Play" is a title taken from *W.B. Yeats: Poems Selected by Seamus Heaney,* "The Road at My Door," from "Meditations in a Time of Civil War" (London: Faber and Faber, 2008). "What Had Once Been My City" refers to Paul Horgan, *Great River: The Rio Grande in North American History* (Middleton, CT: Wesleyan University, 1984), who quotes Don Juan de Oñate y Salazar, colonial governor of Santa Fe de Nuevo Mexico who was noted for the destruction of Acoma Pueblo and vicious cruelty to its survivors. "A Compelling Velvety Voice" quotes Roberto Bolaño, *Antwerp,* tr. Natasha Wimmer (New York: New Directions, 2002).

Acknowledgments

Thanks to the journal editors who gave a place to these poems:

The Antioch Review, "The Mouth with the Gold Teeth Speaks," "Evidently I Was
Still Somewhere."

Archipelago, "Black Cloth Far Away Stays with Me."

Circulo de Poesía, "A Compelling Velvety Voice," "What Had Once
Been My City," in Spanish.

Denver Quarterly, "A Compelling Velvety Voice," "Premonitions and Warnings
We Give Ourselves."

Enchanting Verses Literary Review, "What Had Once Been My City."

Levure Littéraire, "A Compelling Velvety Voice," "The Mouth with the
Gold Teeth Speaks," "Our Lady of Sorrows or Is It Solitude."

Michigan Quarterly Review, "When I'm Gone It's Finished, the Woman One of
65 Speakers of Kumeyaay."

Poetry Flash, "Dark Red and Green."

Pratik, "As Though to Die by Gunshot Were the Finest Thing."

Spillway, "The Sun Stabbing the Water the Wind Tugging at Her Dress,"
"Necrotopography."

Terminus, [The Overland Trail lined with graves], [Pink torn scarves
the sky's antidespair].

Taos Journal of International Poetry and Art, from "Black Cloth Far Away
Stays with Me."

Volt, "News from the Neighborhood of the Cave," "Her Nonchalant Way
of Holding the Glass."

"Half-Unpacked Suitcase," "All Deliberation Ceased," and "The Old Talpa Road," *Casita Poems—An Anthology* (San Francisco: Jambu Press, forthcoming).

"The Pilgrim" appeared in the installation "Storia della Storia" by Sze Tsung Nicolás Leong and Judy Chung, which was part of the exhibition Cinque Mostre 2019 at the American Academy in Rome; it accompanied photographs by Leong and texts by various authors curated and translated by Chung.

"Our Lady of Sorrows or Is It Solitude," Coiled Serpent: Poets Arising from the Cultural Quakes & Shifts in Los Angeles (Los Angeles: Tia Chucha Press, 2016).

"Explicit Comments About the West Coast, Non-Metaphorical," limited edition boxed set of 20 8-page books produced annually by Darin Klein, Los Angeles (fall 2012).

I thank Andrea Watson for her tireless dedication to the writers she publishes. I am grateful to Lesley Cox for her arresting book design. Brian Shields generously gave permission to use his painting on the cover.

This same support was offered to me by the Helene Wurlitzer Foundation, and I thank its director Nic Knight and director emeritus Michael Knight for having brought me to the High Desert. Joan Ryan generously housed me in Taos for almost as long a time as the Wurlitzer. Others who welcomed and housed me were Mara Lonner and Michael Grodsky, and Allan Packer.

For tangibly making the book possible in other ways, I am especially grateful to first readers Gail Wronsky and Leslie Ullman, and to Elena Karina Byrne and Susan Terris. I also was fortunate to have other fine writers as manuscript readers—Molly Bendall, Noah Blaustein, Johanna Drucker, Thaisa Frank, Ramón García, Veronica Golos, Judy Juanita, Katherine McNamara, Sawnie Morris, Linda Lightsey Rice, Catherine Strisik, Judith Taylor, Lynne Thompson, Marci Vogel, and Reed Wilson. My humorous and arty family makes the going much easier—Anna Skinner, David Skinner, Raffi Kevorkian, Maral Mardinos, Ellina Kevorkian, Greg Eklund, Soseh Kevorkian, and, not at all least, Dell Upton.

About The Author

Karen Kevorkian is the author of two poetry collections, *White Stucco Black Wing* and *Lizard Dream*. Her work appears in literary journals including *The Antioch Review, Michigan Quarterly Review, Denver Quarterly, Colorado Review, Los Angeles Review of Books, Virginia Quarterly Review,* and *The Massachusetts Review.* She received fellowships from the Helene Wurlitzer Foundation, the MacDowell Colony, the Millay Colony, the Ucross Foundation, and the Djerassi Foundation. Born in San Antonio, Texas, she studied at the University of Texas, Austin, the University of Virginia, and the University of Utah. She lives in Los Angeles where she is a lecturer at UCLA.

About The Artist

Brian Shields' life and work are an exploration and expression of nature—whether in the wilds of the Rocky Mountains, the policy boardrooms of the US Congress, or in the privacy of his studio. Born into an international artistic family, Shields' art has been influenced by his origins in Barcelona, Spain, and his extensive travels throughout Europe, North America, and Japan. Prior to establishing his home and studio in the mountains of northern New Mexico, he studied and worked in theatre and visual arts in Paris and New York. Shields went on to become a wilderness guide, leading river, mountain, and canyon expeditions throughout the southern Rocky Mountains and the Colorado Plateau, and in 1988 became the founder and director of *Amigos Bravos: Because Water Matters,* a nationally recognized advocacy organization for the protection and restoration of the waters of New Mexico. While continuing his environmental advocacy, Shields is dedicated full time to his studio art practice. Shields exhibits in Los Angeles, Denver, Taos, and Barcelona. He lives with his wife, poet Sawnie Morris, in Ranchos de Taos, New Mexico.

Also By 3: A Taos Press

Collecting Life: Poets On Objects
Known and Imagined
Madelyn Garner & Andrea Watson

Seven
Sheryl Luna

The Luminosity
Bonnie Rose Marcus

3 A. M.
Phyllis Hotch

Trembling in the Bones:
A Commemorative Issue
Eleanor Swanson

Ears of Corn: Listen
Max Early

Elemental
Bill Brown

Rootwork
Veronica Golos

Farolito
Karen S. Córdova

Godwit
Eva Hooker

The Ledgerbook
William S. Barnes

The Mistress
Catherine Strisik

Library of Small Happiness
Leslie Ullman

Day of Clean Brightness
Jane Lin

Bloodline
Radha Marcum

Hum of Our Blood
Madelyn Garner

Dark Ladies & Other Avatars
Joan Roberta Ryan

The Doctor of Flowers
Rachel Blum

Bird Forgiveness
Melinda Palacio

Turquoise Door
Lauren Camp

The Cairns: New and Selected Poems
Bill Brown

We Are Meant To Carry Water
Tina Carlson, Stella Reed &
Katherine Dibella Seluja

The Unbuttoned Eye
Robert Carr

The Burnings
Gary Worth Moody

Girl
Veronica Golos